EMMANUEL JOSEPH

Whispers of the Unfinished, Embracing Growth, Creativity, and the Beauty of Becoming

Copyright © 2025 by Emmanuel Joseph

All rights reserved. No part of this publication may be reproduced, stored or transmitted in any form or by any means, electronic, mechanical, photocopying, recording, scanning, or otherwise without written permission from the publisher. It is illegal to copy this book, post it to a website, or distribute it by any other means without permission.

First edition

This book was professionally typeset on Reedsy.
Find out more at reedsy.com

Contents

1	Chapter 1: The Call to Adventure	1
2	Chapter 2: Embracing Uncertainty	3
3	Chapter 3: The Art of Self-Reflection	5
4	Chapter 4: Cultivating Creativity	7
5	Chapter 5: The Power of Resilience	9
6	Chapter 6: Embracing Vulnerability	11
7	Chapter 7: The Joy of Lifelong Learning	13
8	Chapter 8: The Dance of Balance	15
9	Chapter 9: The Power of Purpose	17
10	Chapter 10: Building Meaningful Connections	19
11	Chapter 11: The Gift of Gratitude	21
12	Chapter 12: The Magic of Mindfulness	23
13	Chapter 13: The Power of Positivity	25
14	Chapter 14: The Beauty of Imperfection	27
15	Chapter 15: The Power of Positivity	29
16	Chapter 16: The Beauty of Imperfection	31
17	Chapter 17: The Legacy of Becoming	33

1

Chapter 1: The Call to Adventure

The allure of the unknown beckons us, tempting the soul to step beyond the confines of familiarity and embark on a journey of transformation. This is the call to adventure, an invitation to leave behind the safety of the shore and sail into uncharted waters. It whispers to the curious heart, promising discoveries that will enrich the essence of our being. While fear of the unknown often holds us back, it is the courage to heed this call that sets the stage for profound growth.

The journey begins with the recognition that the status quo is no longer sufficient. The yearning for something more propels us to take that first, often daunting, step into the realm of possibilities. We may not fully understand what lies ahead, but the pursuit of growth demands that we trust the process. Along this path, we encounter challenges that test our resolve, yet it is through these trials that we uncover our latent potential and the strength to rise above.

As we navigate the twists and turns of our journey, we begin to see the world through a new lens. The obstacles that once seemed insurmountable become opportunities for learning and growth. Each step forward, no matter how small, is a victory that brings us closer to the realization of our true selves. The call to adventure is not just a journey of external exploration, but an inner voyage that reveals the depths of our character and the boundless capacity for transformation.

The first chapter closes with the understanding that the call to adventure is a perpetual echo in our lives. It is the voice that reminds us to keep striving, to never settle for mediocrity, and to embrace the beauty of becoming. With every new beginning, we reaffirm our commitment to the journey, knowing that the whispers of the unfinished are guiding us towards a destiny rich with growth, creativity, and the promise of what is yet to come.

2

Chapter 2: Embracing Uncertainty

Life's journey is fraught with uncertainties, and it is through embracing these unknowns that we truly learn to live. The very essence of growth lies in our ability to navigate the ever-changing landscape of existence. To embrace uncertainty is to acknowledge that life is a continuous evolution, where every moment presents an opportunity for discovery and self-improvement. The beauty of becoming lies in the willingness to dance with the unknown and to find solace in the unpredictability of our journey.

When we let go of the need for certainty, we open ourselves up to a world of endless possibilities. The fear of the unknown can be paralyzing, but it is through facing this fear that we find the courage to take risks and make bold decisions. It is in the moments of uncertainty that we learn to trust our instincts and to rely on our inner strength. By embracing uncertainty, we become more adaptable and resilient, better equipped to handle the challenges that life throws our way.

In the midst of uncertainty, creativity flourishes. When we step into the unknown, we are forced to think outside the box and to come up with innovative solutions to the problems we encounter. This process of creative problem-solving not only helps us overcome obstacles but also fuels our personal and professional growth. Embracing uncertainty allows us to see the world from different perspectives, fostering empathy and understanding as we navigate the complexities of human existence.

The chapter concludes with a reflection on the importance of embracing uncertainty as a means of personal growth. By learning to find comfort in the unknown, we become more open to new experiences and more willing to take the necessary steps toward self-improvement. The journey of becoming is one of continuous exploration, where the whispers of the unfinished guide us toward a future full of promise and potential. In embracing uncertainty, we find the courage to live authentically and to create a life that is a true reflection of our innermost desires.

3

Chapter 3: The Art of Self-Reflection

Self-reflection is a powerful tool that allows us to understand our innermost thoughts, feelings, and motivations. It is through this process that we gain insight into our strengths and weaknesses, and develop a deeper understanding of our true selves. Self-reflection is an ongoing practice, one that requires honesty and vulnerability. By taking the time to reflect on our experiences and emotions, we can identify patterns and behaviors that may be holding us back, and make conscious decisions to change and grow.

The practice of self-reflection often begins with asking ourselves probing questions. What are my core values? What drives me? What are my fears and how do they influence my actions? These questions help us to uncover the underlying beliefs and assumptions that shape our behavior. By examining our thoughts and emotions, we can begin to recognize the impact they have on our lives and make informed choices about how to move forward.

In addition to self-examination, self-reflection also involves seeking feedback from others. By inviting trusted friends, family members, or mentors to share their perspectives, we gain valuable insights that can help us see ourselves more clearly. Constructive feedback allows us to identify blind spots and areas for improvement, and encourages us to continue growing and evolving. The willingness to listen and learn from others is a hallmark of true self-awareness.

The chapter concludes with a reminder that self-reflection is a lifelong journey. It is not a one-time event, but a continuous process of introspection and growth. By regularly engaging in self-reflection, we become more attuned to our inner world and better equipped to navigate the complexities of life. The whispers of the unfinished call us to embrace this practice, guiding us towards a deeper understanding of ourselves and the beauty of becoming.

4

Chapter 4: Cultivating Creativity

Creativity is the spark that ignites innovation and brings new ideas to life. It is the ability to see the world through fresh eyes and to approach problems with an open mind. Cultivating creativity involves nurturing our innate curiosity and allowing ourselves the freedom to explore and experiment. It is through this process that we discover our unique talents and develop the skills to express ourselves in new and meaningful ways.

One of the key aspects of cultivating creativity is creating an environment that fosters inspiration and imagination. This may involve surrounding ourselves with diverse perspectives, engaging in activities that stimulate our senses, or simply allowing ourselves time to daydream and explore new ideas. By creating space for creativity, we open ourselves up to new possibilities and encourage the flow of innovative thought.

Another important aspect of creativity is the willingness to take risks and embrace failure. Not every idea will be a success, and not every attempt will lead to a breakthrough. However, it is through the process of trial and error that we learn and grow. By embracing failure as a natural part of the creative process, we build resilience and develop the confidence to keep pushing the boundaries of what is possible.

The chapter concludes with a reflection on the importance of cultivating creativity as a means of personal and professional growth. Creativity is not limited to the arts; it is a mindset that can be applied to all areas of life. By nurturing our creative spirit, we enhance our ability to think critically, solve problems, and adapt to change. The whispers of the unfinished remind us that creativity is a vital component of the journey of becoming, and that through it, we can create a life that is rich with meaning and purpose.

5

Chapter 5: The Power of Resilience

Resilience is the ability to bounce back from adversity and to persevere in the face of challenges. It is a quality that enables us to navigate the ups and downs of life with grace and determination. Resilience is not about avoiding difficulties, but about facing them head-on and emerging stronger on the other side. It is through the trials and tribulations that we develop the strength and fortitude to keep moving forward.

The journey of resilience begins with a mindset that embraces challenges as opportunities for growth. When we encounter obstacles, we have a choice: to be defeated by them or to use them as stepping stones to greater heights. By adopting a positive attitude and focusing on solutions rather than problems, we cultivate the resilience needed to overcome adversity. This mindset allows us to see setbacks as temporary and to maintain hope and optimism even in the darkest of times.

Another key aspect of resilience is the support of a strong social network. Friends, family, and mentors play a crucial role in helping us navigate difficult situations. They provide encouragement, guidance, and a listening ear, reminding us that we are not alone in our struggles. Building and maintaining meaningful connections with others not only enhances our resilience but also enriches our lives with love and companionship.

The chapter concludes with a reflection on the importance of self-care in building resilience. Taking care of our physical, emotional, and mental well-being is essential for maintaining the strength and energy needed to face life's challenges. This includes practices such as regular exercise, healthy eating, mindfulness, and seeking professional help when needed. By prioritizing self-care, we build a solid foundation for resilience, enabling us to navigate the journey of becoming with confidence and grace.

6

Chapter 6: Embracing Vulnerability

Vulnerability is often seen as a weakness, but in reality, it is a powerful strength that allows us to connect with others on a deeper level. Embracing vulnerability means being open and honest about our true selves, including our fears, insecurities, and imperfections. It is through this openness that we build authentic relationships and foster a sense of belonging.

The journey of embracing vulnerability begins with self-acceptance. We must acknowledge and accept our flaws and limitations, recognizing that they are an inherent part of the human experience. By embracing our imperfections, we free ourselves from the burden of trying to be perfect and allow ourselves to be truly seen. This self-acceptance is the foundation of vulnerability, enabling us to show up as our authentic selves in all aspects of our lives.

Embracing vulnerability also involves taking risks and stepping out of our comfort zones. It means being willing to face rejection, failure, and criticism in pursuit of our dreams and aspirations. By taking these risks, we demonstrate courage and resilience, and we open ourselves up to new opportunities and experiences. Vulnerability is not about being reckless, but about being willing to take calculated risks in the name of growth and self-discovery.

The chapter concludes with a reflection on the power of vulnerability in building connections with others. When we allow ourselves to be vulnerable, we invite others to do the same. This creates a space for mutual understanding, empathy, and support. By embracing vulnerability, we deepen our relationships and create a sense of community and belonging. The whispers of the unfinished remind us that vulnerability is an essential part of the journey of becoming, and that through it, we find the courage to live authentically and connect with others on a meaningful level.

7

Chapter 7: The Joy of Lifelong Learning

Lifelong learning is an ongoing, voluntary, and self-motivated pursuit of knowledge for personal or professional reasons. It is the continuous quest for improvement and growth, driven by a deep-seated curiosity and a desire to understand the world around us. Lifelong learning is not confined to formal education; it encompasses all experiences and opportunities that contribute to our personal and intellectual development.

The journey of lifelong learning begins with a mindset that values curiosity and exploration. It is about maintaining an open mind and a willingness to seek out new knowledge and experiences. This mindset allows us to view every moment as a learning opportunity, whether it is through reading books, engaging in conversations, or exploring new hobbies. By embracing this mindset, we cultivate a sense of wonder and excitement that fuels our desire to learn and grow.

Lifelong learning also involves setting goals and creating a plan for achieving them. This may include identifying areas of interest, seeking out resources, and dedicating time and effort to the pursuit of knowledge. By setting clear goals, we create a roadmap for our learning journey and ensure that we stay focused and motivated. This process of goal-setting and planning also helps us to measure our progress and celebrate our achievements along the way.

The chapter concludes with a reflection on the importance of lifelong learning in the journey of becoming. By continuously seeking out new knowledge and experiences, we keep our minds sharp and our spirits invigorated. Lifelong learning enriches our lives with new perspectives and insights, and empowers us to navigate the complexities of the modern world. The whispers of the unfinished remind us that the journey of becoming is a lifelong endeavor, and that through the joy of learning, we can create a life that is vibrant, meaningful, and fulfilling.

8

Chapter 8: The Dance of Balance

Balance is the harmonious integration of various aspects of our lives, allowing us to navigate the demands of work, relationships, and personal well-being with grace and ease. It is the delicate dance of finding equilibrium amidst the chaos, and creating a sense of stability and peace. The pursuit of balance is an ongoing journey, one that requires mindfulness, intention, and a deep understanding of our priorities and values.

The journey of balance begins with self-awareness. We must first understand our own needs, desires, and limitations in order to create a life that is aligned with our values and goals. This involves regularly checking in with ourselves and assessing how we are feeling physically, emotionally, and mentally. By cultivating self-awareness, we can identify areas of imbalance and make conscious choices to restore harmony in our lives.

Another key aspect of balance is setting boundaries and learning to say no. It is essential to recognize our own limits and to prioritize our well-being above all else. This may involve setting clear boundaries with others, delegating tasks, or simply taking time for ourselves. By honoring our own needs and respecting our boundaries, we create a foundation of balance that allows us to show up fully in all areas of our lives.

The chapter concludes with a reflection on the importance of balance in the journey of becoming. By creating a life that is balanced and harmonious, we cultivate a sense of inner peace and stability that supports our growth and development. The whispers of the unfinished remind us that balance is not a destination, but a continuous process of adjustment and realignment. Through the dance of balance, we find the strength and resilience to navigate the challenges of life and to embrace the beauty of becoming.

9

Chapter 9: The Power of Purpose

Finding our purpose is a journey of self-discovery that involves uncovering our passions, values, and aspirations. It is through this process that we gain a deeper understanding of what drives us and what gives our lives meaning. Purpose is the guiding star that illuminates our path and provides us with a sense of direction and fulfillment.

The journey of discovering our purpose begins with introspection. We must take the time to reflect on our experiences, strengths, and interests, and consider how they align with our values and goals. This may involve exploring new activities, seeking out mentors, and asking ourselves probing questions. What brings me joy? What am I passionate about? What impact do I want to have on the world? By answering these questions, we gain insight into our purpose and the unique contribution we can make.

Purpose is not a fixed destination, but an evolving journey. As we grow and change, our purpose may shift and take on new forms. It is important to remain open to new possibilities and to continuously reassess our goals and aspirations. By staying true to our core values and passions, we can navigate the twists and turns of life with a sense of purpose and direction.

The chapter concludes with a reflection on the importance of living a purpose-driven life. When we are aligned with our purpose, we experience a greater sense of fulfillment and satisfaction. Our actions become more intentional, and we are better equipped to overcome challenges and stay motivated. The whispers of the unfinished remind us that the journey of becoming is one of continuous exploration and growth, and that through the pursuit of our purpose, we can create a life that is rich with meaning and impact.

10

Chapter 10: Building Meaningful Connections

Meaningful connections are the foundation of a fulfilling and enriching life. It is through our relationships with others that we experience love, support, and a sense of belonging. Building meaningful connections requires effort, vulnerability, and a genuine interest in understanding and supporting others.

The journey of building meaningful connections begins with being present and attentive. We must be fully engaged in our interactions, actively listening and showing empathy towards others. This involves putting aside distractions and giving our full attention to the person in front of us. By being present, we create a space for authentic and meaningful conversations that deepen our relationships.

Another key aspect of building meaningful connections is vulnerability. When we allow ourselves to be open and honest about our true selves, we invite others to do the same. This creates a space for mutual understanding and trust, and strengthens the bond between us. Vulnerability is not about oversharing, but about being willing to share our thoughts, feelings, and experiences in a way that fosters connection and intimacy.

The chapter concludes with a reflection on the importance of nurturing and maintaining meaningful connections. Relationships require ongoing effort and commitment, and it is important to regularly invest time and energy into our connections. By showing appreciation, offering support, and being there for others, we create a network of meaningful relationships that enrich our lives and provide us with a sense of belonging. The whispers of the unfinished remind us that the journey of becoming is one of interconnectedness, and that through building and nurturing meaningful connections, we can create a life that is rich with love and support.

11

Chapter 11: The Gift of Gratitude

Gratitude is a powerful practice that allows us to appreciate the beauty and abundance in our lives. It is the simple act of recognizing and acknowledging the good things we have, and expressing our appreciation for them. Gratitude has the power to transform our perspective, shifting our focus from what is lacking to what is abundant. It is through the practice of gratitude that we cultivate a sense of contentment and joy.

The journey of gratitude begins with mindfulness. We must be present in the moment and fully aware of the blessings that surround us. This may involve taking time each day to reflect on the things we are grateful for, whether it is the support of loved ones, the beauty of nature, or the small moments of joy that brighten our days. By consciously focusing on the positive aspects of our lives, we train our minds to see the world through a lens of abundance and appreciation.

Gratitude also involves expressing our appreciation to others. By acknowledging the contributions and kindness of those around us, we strengthen our relationships and create a sense of connection and belonging. This may involve writing thank-you notes, offering verbal expressions of gratitude, or performing acts of kindness in return. When we express our gratitude, we not only enhance our own well-being but also spread positivity and joy to others.

The chapter concludes with a reflection on the transformative power of gratitude in the journey of becoming. By cultivating an attitude of gratitude, we open our hearts to the beauty and abundance that life has to offer. Gratitude helps us to navigate challenges with a positive mindset and to appreciate the small victories along the way. The whispers of the unfinished remind us that gratitude is an essential part of the journey of becoming, and that through it, we can create a life that is rich with contentment and joy.

12

Chapter 12: The Magic of Mindfulness

Mindfulness is the practice of being fully present in the moment, without judgment or distraction. It is the ability to bring our attention to the here and now, and to engage with our experiences with a sense of openness and curiosity. Mindfulness allows us to cultivate a deeper awareness of our thoughts, emotions, and sensations, and to respond to them with clarity and compassion.

The journey of mindfulness begins with the practice of meditation. By setting aside time each day to sit quietly and focus on our breath, we train our minds to become more present and attentive. Meditation helps us to develop a sense of inner calm and stability, and to become more aware of the patterns of our thoughts and emotions. Through regular practice, we learn to observe our experiences without getting caught up in them, and to respond to them with greater clarity and intention.

Mindfulness also involves bringing a sense of presence and awareness to our daily activities. Whether it is eating a meal, taking a walk, or engaging in a conversation, we can practice mindfulness by paying full attention to the present moment. This means setting aside distractions and fully engaging with our experiences, allowing ourselves to be fully immersed in the here and now. By practicing mindfulness in our daily lives, we cultivate a sense of presence and connection that enhances our overall well-being.

The chapter concludes with a reflection on the importance of mindfulness in the journey of becoming. By cultivating mindfulness, we develop a deeper understanding of ourselves and our experiences, and we become more attuned to the present moment. Mindfulness helps us to navigate challenges with a sense of clarity and composure, and to appreciate the beauty and richness of each moment. The whispers of the unfinished remind us that mindfulness is an essential part of the journey of becoming, and that through it, we can create a life that is rich with presence and awareness.

13

Chapter 13: The Power of Positivity

Positivity is a powerful force that has the ability to transform our mindset and our lives. It is the practice of focusing on the good in any situation, and approaching life with an optimistic and hopeful attitude. Positivity does not mean ignoring the challenges and difficulties we face, but rather choosing to see the opportunities for growth and learning that they present.

The journey of positivity begins with our thoughts. Our minds are incredibly powerful, and the way we think about our experiences has a profound impact on how we feel and act. By consciously choosing to focus on the positive aspects of any situation, we can shift our mindset and create a more optimistic outlook. This may involve practicing gratitude, reframing negative thoughts, and surrounding ourselves with positive influences.

Positivity also involves taking action to create a positive environment. This may include setting goals, engaging in activities that bring us joy, and building relationships with supportive and uplifting people. By creating a positive environment, we enhance our overall well-being and create a foundation for happiness and success. Positivity is contagious, and by spreading positivity to others, we create a ripple effect that can have a profound impact on our communities and the world.

The chapter concludes with a reflection on the importance of positivity in the journey of becoming. By cultivating a positive mindset and creating a positive environment, we empower ourselves to overcome challenges and achieve our goals. Positivity helps us to navigate the ups and downs of life with grace and resilience, and to appreciate the beauty and abundance that surrounds us. The whispers of the unfinished remind us that positivity is an essential part of the journey of becoming, and that through it, we can create a life that is rich with hope and joy.

14

Chapter 14: The Beauty of Imperfection

Imperfection is an inherent part of the human experience, and it is through embracing our imperfections that we truly learn to live authentically. The pursuit of perfection can be a source of stress and frustration, as we strive to meet unrealistic standards and expectations. However, it is through accepting and embracing our imperfections that we find freedom and self-acceptance.

The journey of embracing imperfection begins with self-compassion. We must learn to be kind and gentle with ourselves, recognizing that we are all imperfect beings on a journey of growth and learning. This means letting go of self-criticism and negative self-talk, and instead, practicing self-love and acceptance. By embracing our imperfections, we free ourselves from the burden of trying to be perfect and allow ourselves to be truly seen.

Embracing imperfection also involves recognizing the beauty and uniqueness that it brings. Our imperfections make us who we are, and they add depth and richness to our lives. By celebrating our quirks and idiosyncrasies, we embrace our authentic selves and create a life that is a true reflection of our individuality. Imperfection is not a flaw, but a gift that allows us to connect with others on a deeper level and to appreciate the diversity of the human experience.

The chapter concludes with a reflection on the importance of embracing imperfection in the journey of becoming. By accepting and celebrating our imperfections, we cultivate a sense of self-acceptance and authenticity that enhances our overall well-being. The whispers of the unfinished remind us that imperfection is an essential part of the journey of becoming, and that through it, we can create a life that is rich with meaning and beauty.

15

Chapter 15: The Power of Positivity

Positivity is a powerful force that has the ability to transform our mindset and our lives. It is the practice of focusing on the good in any situation, and approaching life with an optimistic and hopeful attitude. Positivity does not mean ignoring the challenges and difficulties we face, but rather choosing to see the opportunities for growth and learning that they present.

The journey of positivity begins with our thoughts. Our minds are incredibly powerful, and the way we think about our experiences has a profound impact on how we feel and act. By consciously choosing to focus on the positive aspects of any situation, we can shift our mindset and create a more optimistic outlook. This may involve practicing gratitude, reframing negative thoughts, and surrounding ourselves with positive influences.

Positivity also involves taking action to create a positive environment. This may include setting goals, engaging in activities that bring us joy, and building relationships with supportive and uplifting people. By creating a positive environment, we enhance our overall well-being and create a foundation for happiness and success. Positivity is contagious, and by spreading positivity to others, we create a ripple effect that can have a profound impact on our communities and the world.

The chapter concludes with a reflection on the importance of positivity in the journey of becoming. By cultivating a positive mindset and creating a positive environment, we empower ourselves to overcome challenges and achieve our goals. Positivity helps us to navigate the ups and downs of life with grace and resilience, and to appreciate the beauty and abundance that surrounds us. The whispers of the unfinished remind us that positivity is an essential part of the journey of becoming, and that through it, we can create a life that is rich with hope and joy.

16

Chapter 16: The Beauty of Imperfection

Imperfection is an inherent part of the human experience, and it is through embracing our imperfections that we truly learn to live authentically. The pursuit of perfection can be a source of stress and frustration, as we strive to meet unrealistic standards and expectations. However, it is through accepting and embracing our imperfections that we find freedom and self-acceptance.

The journey of embracing imperfection begins with self-compassion. We must learn to be kind and gentle with ourselves, recognizing that we are all imperfect beings on a journey of growth and learning. This means letting go of self-criticism and negative self-talk, and instead, practicing self-love and acceptance. By embracing our imperfections, we free ourselves from the burden of trying to be perfect and allow ourselves to be truly seen.

Embracing imperfection also involves recognizing the beauty and uniqueness that it brings. Our imperfections make us who we are, and they add depth and richness to our lives. By celebrating our quirks and idiosyncrasies, we embrace our authentic selves and create a life that is a true reflection of our individuality. Imperfection is not a flaw, but a gift that allows us to connect with others on a deeper level and to appreciate the diversity of the human experience.

The chapter concludes with a reflection on the importance of embracing imperfection in the journey of becoming. By accepting and celebrating our imperfections, we cultivate a sense of self-acceptance and authenticity that enhances our overall well-being. The whispers of the unfinished remind us that imperfection is an essential part of the journey of becoming, and that through it, we can create a life that is rich with meaning and beauty.

17

Chapter 17: The Legacy of Becoming

Legacy is the enduring impact we leave on the world, the mark we make that lives on beyond our time. It is the culmination of our values, actions, and the lives we've touched. Building a legacy is not about seeking recognition or fame, but about creating a lasting positive influence that reflects the essence of who we are and what we stand for.

The journey of building a legacy begins with intentionality. We must live each day with purpose and a clear understanding of the values that guide us. This involves making conscious choices that align with our principles and contribute to the greater good. By living with intention, we create a foundation for a legacy that is rooted in authenticity and integrity.

Another key aspect of legacy is the impact we have on others. Our relationships, acts of kindness, and contributions to our communities all play a part in shaping our legacy. By fostering meaningful connections and uplifting those around us, we create a ripple effect that extends far beyond our immediate sphere. The way we inspire, support, and empower others becomes a testament to our life's work.

The chapter concludes with a reflection on the significance of legacy in the journey of becoming. As we navigate the path of growth and self-discovery, we are constantly shaping the legacy we will leave behind. The whispers of the unfinished remind us that our legacy is not defined by a single moment, but by the accumulation of our experiences, choices, and the love we share.

Through the legacy of becoming, we create a lasting impact that continues to inspire and uplift future generations.

Book Description: Whispers of the Unfinished: Embracing Growth, Creativity, and the Beauty of Becoming

"Whispers of the Unfinished: Embracing Growth, Creativity, and the Beauty of Becoming" is a transformative journey into the heart of personal development and self-discovery. This book invites readers to explore the profound insights and wisdom that emerge from the process of growth and transformation. Through 17 thoughtfully crafted chapters, the book delves into the core aspects of embracing uncertainty, cultivating creativity, building resilience, and finding purpose in life's journey.

Each chapter offers a deep and reflective exploration of themes such as self-reflection, gratitude, mindfulness, vulnerability, and the power of positivity. With engaging narratives and practical insights, the book encourages readers to embrace their imperfections, build meaningful connections, and navigate the complexities of life with grace and authenticity. The whispers of the unfinished guide readers towards a richer understanding of themselves and the world around them, fostering a sense of continuous growth and becoming.

"Whispers of the Unfinished" is a celebration of the beauty of the human experience, and a reminder that the journey of becoming is a lifelong adventure filled with opportunities for growth, creativity, and self-discovery. It is an inspiring and uplifting read for anyone seeking to deepen their understanding of themselves and to create a life that is rich with meaning and purpose. Through the pages of this book, readers are invited to listen to the whispers of the unfinished and to embrace the limitless possibilities that lie ahead.

www.ingramcontent.com/pod-product-compliance
Ingram Content Group UK Ltd.
Pitfield, Milton Keynes, MK11 3LW, UK
UKHW022140120325
456116UK00013B/299